You've learned about things like recycling and turning off the lights. That's important, but there are even bigger things that you can do to help our Earth. Like using your voice.

Read this guide to learn all you can, so you can teach people what you know.

+1°C

What's going on with our Earth?

The temperature on the surface of our Earth is going up. In fact, it is 1 °C (1.8 °F) warmer. Scientists call this **"global warming"** and it's making things harder for everyone.

It's not too late.

But we need to get started.

Just start.

"Our Earth doesn't need you to be perfect.

It just needs you to start.

Until someone builds plastic-free helmets, you'll need to wear a plastic one when you ride a bike or play football.

Even though natural gas heats your town's swimming pool, you should still have fun swimming in it.

If you have to take an airplane because there's no other way to get there, don't worry.

Fixing everything won't happen for a while.

Kids should just do their best.

And teach adults what they know in the meantime."

Matthew N. Age 15, Boston, Massachusetts

Why is it getting warmer?

Although it may be hard to tell that it's warmer when you go outside, our Earth can tell. It's like our Earth has a fever and just a tiny increase in temperature is making it feel lousy. This *fever* triggers wild weather.

Scientists say our Earth is getting warmer because people are doing things to harm it.

But not everyone knows and understands this. Lots of adults did not learn this when they were in school.

+1°C

THE WEATHER GETS WORSE AS TEMPERATURE GOES UP

Our Earth's fever produces wild weather.

See how the temperature gets warmer and it triggers crazy weather? This is what we mean when we say "**climate change.**"

Your mission:

Teach 5 Adults what you learn in this book!

Grown-ups might not even realize the stuff they're doing is hurting our planet.

When you teach others, you can help us save our Earth.

When you see this badge, you'll know it's stuff that adults need to know!

Teach
5
Adults

Why do we need kids to teach adults?

If one person decides to buy potatoes without using a plastic bag, then one plastic bag isn't necessary.

But what if potato companies stopped putting potatoes in plastic bags? Then we wouldn't have **millions** of plastic bags harming our Earth.

Maybe you don't know an adult who works at a potato company. But, you might know a teacher, principal, coach, or parent who makes rules at their job that can help save our Earth.

By teaching someone, *your message spreads so that BIG changes can happen.*

Here's a fun way you can help today...
well, technically tonight:

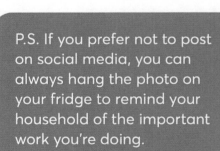

Take the Bedtime Story Challenge.

It's not what you think. (Or maybe it is, because you've definitely already noticed the picture on this page.) If you choose to take this challenge you are going to read to your grown-up. This book. As a bedtime story. We know it'll be great.

Make sure to get a good photo of the moment. Then ask your grown-up to post it on social media, saying something like: *"Best bedtime story ever! I learned about climate change tonight."*

Add the hashtag **#GenerationCarbon**.

This will help to spread the word, so we can all help to save our planet.

P.S. If you prefer not to post on social media, you can always hang the photo on your fridge to remind your household of the important work you're doing.

Or talk about it. "I read my grown-up a bedtime story last night," is a fun way to get someone's attention.

Are you ready to learn all you can about climate change?

What is carbon?

It's inside a pencil, but it's also in the air and in your body. Carbon is in just about everything.

If we burn something with carbon in it, it's released into the air and becomes a gas called carbon dioxide.

You can see carbon when there's smoke coming from a fire, but you can't see it when it's in the form of carbon dioxide.

We've been burning a lot of carbon for about the last hundred years, and now it's become a huge problem.

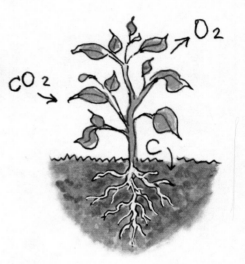

Plants absorb carbon dioxide and change it into oxygen that humans can breathe. But they can't handle the amount of carbon dioxide we're releasing by burning too much fossil fuel.

What are fossil fuels?

400 million years ago

100 million years ago

PRESSURE

HEAT   CRUDE OIL

Tiny plants and animals that contain carbon die.

Under the sand and mud, the dead plants and animals decay.

Crude oil and natural gas are formed and contain lots of carbon.

Fossils are the bones and parts of animals and plants that get turned into a special kind of rock.

Like fossils, crude oil, coal, and natural gas are formed deep in the Earth from the remains of plants, animals, and other living things from long ago.

This is why we call crude oil, coal, and natural gas **fossil fuels**.

We're burning fossil fuels and making a mess.

Let's talk about those fossil fuels.

Coal is often burned to make electricity. When coal is burned, the carbon that's stored in the coal, goes into the air. We call this "releasing carbon."

Crude oil is an ingredient in gasoline that powers cars. When we ride in gas-powered cars, we release carbon too.

Natural gas heats and cools many of our homes. When we turn up the heat, guess what's released? More carbon.

This is important for you to know for your mission.

People release carbon every single day.

There are tons of ways people add too much carbon dioxide to the air. Because carbon dioxide is invisible, we don't always realize the harm we're causing to our Earth.

This is a huge problem. If people could see carbon dioxide, we'd probably be acting faster.

How much carbon are people releasing?

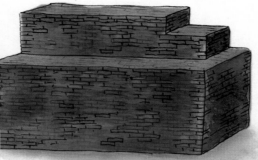

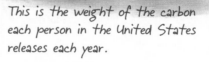

This is the weight of the carbon each person in the United States releases each year.

Goal by 2050: release this weight of carbon.

People reducing their own carbon is helpful, but that won't be enough.

We'll need all kinds of teamwork, inventions, and even new laws if we want to get to 440 bricks.

Each American releases about 14 metric tons of carbon emissions every single year — *that's the weight of 6,300 bricks!*

Scientists say we must reduce the carbon we're releasing to the weight of only 440 bricks. This will mean some BIG changes for all of us.

We can make these changes if we work together.

It's kind of like our planet is holding its breath.

If you've ever tried to swim under water, you know what it's like to hold your breath. It's not comfortable. This is because your body starts to run low on good stuff (oxygen) and fill with not-so-good stuff (carbon dioxide). Your body needs to exhale the carbon dioxide to get rid of it, before it can fill up with oxygen again.

This is why the second you're back above water your mouth opens to breathe. Your body was designed to do this. It needs the oxygen in fresh air. And it needs it as fast as it can get it, so you can feel better and stay healthy.

Carbon overload!

Our planet needs fresh air to stay healthy too. Things like trees and soil and oceans act like sponges to help. They absorb carbon dioxide from the air. But right now, the sponges are almost full.

When people burn fossil fuels, they're releasing too much carbon for the trees and oceans to soak up.

The greenhouse effect.

In 30 A.D., a Roman king requested cucumbers for breakfast. When it was too cold to grow cucumbers outside, the King's servants built the first greenhouse. A greenhouse allows light from the Sun to go through its glass roof, so plants have the light they need to grow. The glass roof also helps keep the heat inside to keep the plants warm. This allows gardeners to grow plants even when it's too cold to grow them outside.

"Mum, it hasn't been raining for so long and it's bad. We need to water the plants in the garden more often."

Matilde R., 8 years old, Bologna, Italy

Sunlight can go through the greenhouse gases.

Greenhouse gases sit here, and trap heat to make our Earth warmer.

Greenhouse gases trap heat.

Greenhouse gases like carbon dioxide act like the glass roof of a greenhouse. Carbon and other gases sit high above the Earth and allow sunlight to reach the Earth. But they also trap the Sun's heat like a greenhouse roof. This is why we call them "greenhouse gases."

This trapped heat is what's warming up our Earth and triggering crazy weather.

When people say "carbon" they could mean any of these greenhouse gases:
- **carbon dioxide** (CO2)
- **methane** (CH4)
- **nitrous oxide** (N2O)
- **water vapor**
- **fluorinated gases**

Greenhouse effect experiment.

Want to learn more about the greenhouse effect? Get ready to move fast, because we're going to set up a race. Between pieces of butter. (We'll give you a minute to read those last few words again.)

Sure, it'll be more like watching Turbo the snail after he lost his special powers than getting to cheer on Lightning McQueen, but we promise it'll be fun. *Ready? Set?*

Materials:
- 2 dark plates or 1 dark cookie sheet
- 2 teaspoons of butter
- 1 clear jar

P.S. If you can't do this activity until later, just skip ahead.

Greenhouse effect experiment.

Go! **Experiment:**

- Place one teaspoon of butter on each of your two plates.

- Place the plates in a sunny spot.

- Cover one of the pieces of butter with the jar.

- Come up with a hypothesis (your best guess!): Which piece of butter will win the race by melting first? (If you really want to do it right, you'll give each piece its very own racing name.)

- See which piece of butter melts first.

Once you're done with your experiment use the butter to spread on your toast. Food waste is also a huge contributor to climate change.

What happened inside the jar?

The covered butter melted first, right? This is the same idea behind the greenhouse effect.

Just like the glass roof of a greenhouse keeps heat inside, the jar kept heat inside of your experiment. On our planet, greenhouse gases act like the jar. They trap the Sun's heat. That's why our Earth is getting warmer.

And that's why it's so important that we race to help our planet.

Ready? Set?
Keep reading...

Our Earth is an ecosystem.

Our Earth is at its best when everything works together. We call this an *ecosystem*.

Right now, our ecosystem is not healthy. It's hard for everything to work together with all of the changes happening to our Earth.

This pond is a healthy ecosystem because everything is working together.

Does this look like a healthy ecosystem to you?

1°C

The climate at ski mountains is usually cold, but because of climate change there's now less snow.

What's weather and what's climate?

What's it like there right now? Sunny? Snowy? You most likely answered fast. Because you know what weather is.

But what about climate? For your mission, it's important to know about both.

Climate is what the weather is usually like in an area over a long time. For example, the climate in Mexico is warm. That's normal in Mexico. The climate in Canada is cooler than Mexico. That's normal there.

"Normal" weather isn't so normal anymore.

Cactus plants grow in warm climates. When it snows in warm places, it's a sign that the climate is changing.

Climate change is, well, changing things. Normal weather is just not happening as often.

In the U.S., Texas had super cold weather in the winter of 2021 that caused pipes to freeze, burst, and flood people's homes. That's not normal.

In Argentina, January 2022 temperatures in Buenos Aires were some of its hottest weather in 115 years. It was so hot that people got really sick. Events like these are happening all over the place.

Have you noticed weird weather where you live?

Teach 5 Adults

"It's probably climate change."

When you hear people talk about these things, remind them, "it's probably climate change."

- Blackouts
- Laggy internet
- Flooded basements
- Frozen gutters
- Cell phone service outages
- Fallen trees
- Potholes
- Cracked pavement
- Asthma
- Allergies
- Fewer ski days
- Mold
- Pollution

- Chubby squirrels
- Disease-carrying mosquitoes
- Wildfires
- Drought
- Heavy downpours
- Heatwaves

Squirrels are getting chubbier because less snow cover allows them to find more food.

"One time, we were going to a baseball game — me and my dad — and right as we got into the stands, it got rained out."

Ivan, Age 8, Minneapolis, MN

What's taking so long to fix climate change?

Climate change has happened slowly. So slowly it's not enough for people to feel warmer when they walk outside. This is one reason people don't know what's happening.

Lately, there have been storms, hurricanes, and heatwaves that help people understand. Some finally realize how much damage has happened to our Earth.

The problem is invisible. You'd be scared if you saw black smoke shooting out of your gas-powered car. But since the greenhouse gases cars release are invisible, it's easy for people to forget the damage they're doing.

Getting people's attention about climate change has been hard. This is why we need you to help.

It's tough because some things that release carbon are things people depend on. Like concrete — making it releases lots of carbon. But in some countries, concrete is used to build lots of houses.

Some people think they'll have to give up doing fun things because of climate change, but that's not true. There are lots of new ways to live that also protect our Earth:

Wind can produce electricity so we can do things like baking cookies.

People can ride *bicycles* to the park instead of driving cars.

Trains are often just as fast as airplanes for your next trip.

ABOUT 82 KG CARBON/PASSENGER

VS

ABOUT 13 KG CARBON/PASSENGER

Landfills.

Every day, people around the world throw away about five million tons of garbage. This is the same weight as 33,000 blue whales. But when you throw something away, it doesn't just "go away." *So, where does it go?*

First, trucks take your garbage to a landfill or garbage dump. A landfill is a big hole dug in the Earth. Garbage trucks dump the trash into the pit, then big machines cover it with dirt.

Keep stuff out of landfills by borrowing stuff you'll only use once. *Did you know that some libraries have tools, cake pans, and games you can borrow?*

The dirt in landfills is home to bacteria that eat the tossed out food, paper, and plastic. As the bacteria eat, they send greenhouse gases such as carbon dioxide and methane into the air. Imagine a gazillion bacteria farts and burps made every second!

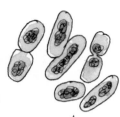

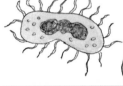

Methane is the greenhouse gas that is released from landfills and traps heat.

More garbage in landfills means more methane in the air. More methane means our Earth gets warmer and our weather gets crazier.

What does plastic have to do with climate change?

Plastic is everywhere. In your shampoo bottle and sneakers. People buy lots of plastic items, often without even thinking. To save our Earth we need companies to stop offering so many plastic items.

Plastic is made from fossil fuels, which release carbon dioxide that warms our Earth. And, believe it or not, most plastic cannot be recycled *even when you put it in a recycling bin.*

One solution is to ask companies to stop using and making plastic — you can usually find their email address on their company's website.

Ask an adult this!

When you were a kid, were there plastic spouts on cardboard milk cartons?

Got a cut on your finger? Since most bandages are made with plastic, you'll need to use one to stop the bleeding.

But wouldn't it be great if companies were only allowed to sell bandages that didn't harm our Earth?

Recycling needs to be fixed.

This is one secret that shouldn't be a secret. Tell everyone!

Most of us have seen the ♻ symbol and try to recycle as much as we can.

We want to let you in on a secret. **Only 8 out of 100 plastic items we put in the recycling bin actually get recycled**. This means the other 92 plastic items we place in the recycle bin are burned, or end up in landfills or the ocean. Recycling 8 bottles is way better than no recycling though!

It takes 400 years to break down plastic. A super long time. As soon as we make one pile of plastic trash, a factory is busy making many more piles of plastic trash. How do factories make plastic? Yep, by burning fossil fuels and releasing even more greenhouse gases into the air.

Spread this news: Most plastic you put in a recycling bin never gets recycled!

Sandwich bags and water bottles that only get used once? We need to stop using those right now.

Toys: an important choice to make when having fun.

Think about the last time you were lucky enough to get a new toy. Chances are, you had to cut through some thick plastic just to get the toy out of its packaging.

As you know, if that plastic went into the trash, it'll take about 400 years to break down. It could even end up in an ocean and hurt fish.

What if instead of collecting more toys, you took more time doing things with your friends like playing tag, taking hikes, and making crafts?

There are all sorts of ways to help. And they all come back to protecting our planet.

Ask your teacher to let you practice writing emails to companies that use lots of plastic packaging. *Be sure to send them photos of the plastic waste.*

Food choices matter.

How do we decide which foods to eat? It has to taste good, that's for sure. But we also eat what's available. Long ago, that meant people only ate what they could grow nearby their homes. This meant they ate root vegetables in the fall or beans and squash in the summertime.

Today, because airplanes can bring us food from around the world, it's possible to get most types of food whenever you want them.

Having so many food choices is nice — but transporting the food in planes and trucks releases a lot of carbon. And having too many choices means food ends up spoiled or simply thrown away.

Teach an adult this! Out of every 10 pounds of food, **3 pounds is wasted!**

Wow your family and friends by mastering tacos, stir fries, and soups. These meals use up lots of bits of food that might otherwise have been wasted.

Food made from animals.

Food made from animals is a big source of greenhouse gases. First, forests are cut down, so animals have land to graze. Cutting down trees releases carbon. And now that trees are cut down, there are fewer trees to absorb carbon.

Then all the animals burp and fart (a lot!). This releases methane, another heat-trapping gas. This makes our Earth warmer and sets off damaging weather.

Choosing to eat fruits and vegetables instead of meat plays a big part in reducing greenhouse gases.

You have the power:
- Choose a veggie burger instead of a beef burger in the cafeteria. You can still add all the ketchup, pickles, and mustard you like!
- Drink plant-based milks like oat or soy instead of dairy.
- Eat more plants: You don't have to become a complete vegetarian, unless you want to.
- Just start by adding more fruits and veggies to your plate.

Recipe for bean burger.

CUMIN 1t

CHILI POWDER 1t

BROWN SUGAR 1t

SALT ½t

PEPPER ½t

cooked RICE 1C

ONION minced, sauteed

1½ C BREADCRUMBS

mix

BLACK BEANS drained

mash

OIL 1T

BBQ SAUCE 3T

t = teaspoon
T = Tablespoon
C = cup

×8

OIL

fry 4 minutes each side

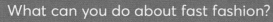

What is fast fashion?

Stores used to display new clothing 4 times a year: Winter, Spring, Summer, and Fall. Now new clothes appear in stores every week — that's 52 times a year! In the last 20 years, the amount of clothing made has doubled.

People want to be stylish, so they buy more new clothes and trash the "old" ones. And we know what happens when something goes to the landfill.

What can you do about fast fashion?
- **Wear hand-me-downs** and share clothes with others.
- Ask adults to **shop at second-hand stores**. Bonus: Second-hand jeans are soft and broken in.
- **Mend clothing** that's ripped.
- **Toss your backpack in the washer** to clean it instead of buying a new one.

Bojo Bandango, courtesy of the 'The Big PickSure Book' by OuiChoose.

Will these animals survive climate change?

Climate change is right here, right now. Every living thing on our planet will be affected. Many animals are already suffering. Some can't have babies. Some can't find food. Others can't live in the warmer temperatures.

Here are just a few of the animals at risk right now:

- Adélie penguins
- African forest elephants
- Asian elephants
- Atlantic puffins
- Bengal tigers
- Black-headed squirrel monkeys
- Bumblebees
- Darwin's frogs
- Duck-billed platypuses
- Emperor penguins
- Green sea turtles
- Hippopotamuses
- Leatherback turtles
- Monarch butterflies
- Mountain gorillas
- North atlantic right whales
- Polar bears
- Snow leopards

And the thousands of bugs and insects you've never heard of.

Check out **thecarbonalmanac.org/genc** to learn more. | 37

Activity:

Follow these steps to draw a green sea turtle.

Share your drawings on social with the hashtag #GenerationCarbon

Climate change causes strong storms that destroy the sea turtles' beaches.

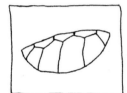
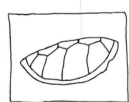
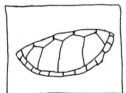
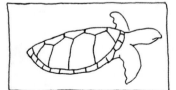
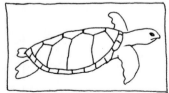
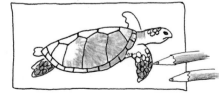

Now try drawing a monarch butterfly.

Share your drawings on social with the hashtag #GenerationCarbon

Warmer temperatures mean monarch butterflies have a hard time surviving.

Introducing net-zero emissions.

This sounds complicated, but it's really simple.

For millions of years when greenhouse gases were released, our Earth soaked up enough of them to keep the planet healthy.

Right now, that's not happening. There are so many greenhouse gases being released that the Earth can't soak them up fast enough. *It just can't keep up!* Remember the full sponges? So that's why we need to work on getting to net zero.

Emissions: a fancy word that means the release of greenhouse gases.

Net-zero emissions: when the Earth can soak up all the greenhouse gases we release.

Balancing greenhouse gases.

When the left and right sides of the scale are at the same level, they are in balance, and we have reached net zero.

Imagine a see-saw or a scale. *On the right of the scale:* things that release greenhouse gases like trucks and plastic bottles. *On the left of the scale:* things that soak up greenhouse gases like trees and oceans.

If all the greenhouse gases released are removed by the trees and oceans, the scale balances, and we've reached **net zero.** By keeping the scale balanced, the Earth stays healthy.

Right now, there are more greenhouse gases than our Earth can handle, so the scale is not balanced. Scientists want us to balance the scale by the year 2050.

How bad is it for our Earth if you...
play some video games?

Most people's doesn't.

Did you know that everything you plug in adds to climate change? This is especially true if your electricity doesn't come from the sun or wind.

A lamp, TV, charging phone – they all release carbon. So does a PlayStation, computer, or anything else you use to play video games. (Not to mention all the plastic it took to make these things.) It's not a lot of carbon, but it's still good for you to know.

Answer: **Not so bad.**

How bad is it for our Earth if you...

get car rides to places you could walk?

A big chunk of the carbon released on our planet comes from vehicles. Cars that run on gas are a part of that. And trucks are even worse. That's why walking and riding a bike help our planet. How we choose to get to places matters.

Answer: **Pretty bad!**

How bad is it for our Earth if you...

eat a cheeseburger?

It's not just about eating the burger — it's about all it took to get the burger to your plate. The food most likely needed machines to be made, and big trucks to get it to stores. Each of those releases a lot of carbon. And before that, there was the cow. Cows need a ton of land and water — so much more than vegetables do. They also burp out methane — a greenhouse gas that traps heat and makes our Earth warmer.

 Answer: **Not so great.**

For now, try to reduce the amount of meat you eat.

What can we do?

How can kids help?

Start anywhere.
Don't worry about
being perfect.

Dry your clothes in the Sun.

Remind your teachers,
class parents, and
coaches:

No camping trip, class
party, or soccer game
needs to include plastic
water bottles!

Plant a vegetable garden
and fruit trees.

When you see things
like bananas wrapped in
plastic, point out to adults
how bananas this is.

Adults don't always see
things the way kids do.

Use a refillable water bottle.
Trucks that transport heavy
water bottles release a lot
of carbon.

*Get The Carbon Almanac for the
adults in your life.* You can borrow it
from the library, or learn more from
thecarbonalmanac.org/genc.

Let's get people's attention!

To get the people you live with to understand what's happening to our Earth too, **post the fast facts on the next page**, on your bathroom wall.

Yes, even your bathroom can be a classroom!

FAST FACTS ABOUT
Climate Change.

- People use coal, oil, and gas for fuel. These *fossil fuels* allow people to drive cars and make electricity.

- Fossil fuels release carbon dioxide into the atmosphere.

- Carbon dioxide traps heat.

- Trapped heat makes our Earth warmer.

- It may not feel warmer outside our door, but just a tiny increase in temperature has a big impact, like serious storms, flooding, and droughts.

- Storms damage buildings, homes, animals, and our Earth.

Download this from **thecarbonalmanac. org/genc**.

BIG changes are needed to stop climate change like:

- **Passing laws against companies from selling things that harm our Earth.**

- **Making electricity from Sun and wind.**

- **Voting for people who can make laws against harming our Earth.**

- **Teaching others about climate change. Lots of people don't know about this stuff.**

You can help reduce the use of fossil fuel:

Reuse plastics

The next time you get a plastic fork, save it and use it over and over again. Plastic is made from fossil fuels, and most people toss plastic after just one use.

Electric vehicles

Is your family buying a new car? Encourage them to consider electric vehicles that need no gasoline.

Sun and wind

Teach an adult this: You can now buy electricity made by 100% Sun and wind. And it's usually not more expensive! Check your local electric company's website to learn how.

"THINK BIG" ideas kids can teach adults.

Teach 5 Adults

YOU can make a difference! Where can you begin to help the planet?

Greta Thunberg, the young Swedish climate activist, changed her parents' minds FIRST. She showed them facts. They watched movies about the environment together.

But the change did not happen right away. Greta kept pushing until the grown-ups REALLY listened. Children are better than grown-ups at making people take action — no surprises there, kids are awesome!

Here's a list of things you can teach some grown-ups.

These actions make a **HUGE** difference!

PLEASE TURN OFF ENGINE while waiting

- Start **a bike-to-school club** to reduce the carbon released by the cars at school drop-offs.

- Have your school officer hang signs **asking drivers to turn off cars when picking up kids.**

- Ask your teacher to make the theme of this year's **science fair all about climate change.**

- **Teach five grown-ups what you know about climate change.** Ask them to teach five more people. See how things can spread?

These are just ideas. Start with anything you can dream up.

Our Earth doesn't need you to be perfect. It just needs you to start.

More actions that make a difference!

- **Turn off the lights you don't need.** Wasted electricity means more carbon that's released.

- **Close doors right away** so heat doesn't escape.

- **Borrow items like jewelry, tools, and games** so factories don't release carbon making new stuff.

- Next time you choose your meal, **choose a veggie burger**. Or make the bean burger recipe from this book.

- Run a class contest to see who can keep their pencil for the longest amount of time. It's important **to not throw things away when they are still useful**. Because carbon is released to make things too.

- **Ask your principal to turn down the heat to instantly reduce the carbon being released**. Especially if kids are wearing shorts in the colder months!

Activity:

Planet-saving craft:
Class T-shirts.

Instructions by **Jodi Levine** for
Generation Carbon: It's time to start.

Bright T-shirts can help your teacher make sure the whole class stays together on a field trip and show your school spirit. But it's not cool to wear a shirt that says, "3rd Graders Rock" when you're in 4th grade. So, class shirts tend to get tossed after just a few wears.

For your next class party or field trip, make these bright class T-shirts. But don't take them home – leave them for your teacher to use year after year. This way, T-shirts will stay out of landfills.

 Show this to your teacher, scout leader, or class parent.

Activity:

Planet-saving craft:
Class T-shirts.

→

Show this to your teacher, scout leader, or class parent.

1

- **Use** a baby potato with a pointy bottom.

- **Cut** it in half with a knife. This will create a teardrop shape. *Kids, please get an adult to help with the cutting.*

2

- **Slide** a cardboard sheet into the T-shirt so the paint won't bleed through to the back.

- **Plan** your shirt design. Use small pieces of masking tape to help plan the spacings.

3

- **Dip** the cut end of the potato into acrylic paint or fabric paint.

- **Stamp** your pattern on the T-shirt! Print twice in a V-shape to create a heart shape.

Jobs that will help save the Earth.

Want to take your mission even further? Great. We need you. Now there are all kinds of ways you can do this.

But let's talk about a big one: When you grow up, you could choose a job that helps to save the Earth.

Here are 5 of them: →

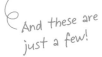

And these are just a few!

Environmental teachers: Teach students what they need to know to protect the planet.

Environmental scientists: Investigate climate change. *(Kind of like an Earth doctor!)*

Park rangers: Protect parks and the people visiting them.

Futurists: Imagine a better world and help people get there!

Eco-Inventors: Create Earth-saving inventions. *(You'll see some of these coming up soon!)*

Be a climate activist.

You could also become a climate activist, which is a name for anyone who takes action to fight climate change. Sometimes this is a job. Other times? It's just something people do. Greta Thunberg decided to take action as a kid. Now at age 19 she is one of the world's most well-known climate activists.

Just like Greta, you don't need to be an adult to be a climate activist. If you wanted, you could become one today.

There are so many things you can do to start making a difference.

Like completing your mission to teach 5 adults about climate change. *You're doing awesome so far!*

"You are never too small to make a difference."

- Greta Thunberg

You can invent things that'll get us out of this mess.

Draw your own eco-invention and share it with us using the hashtag **#GenerationCarbon**.

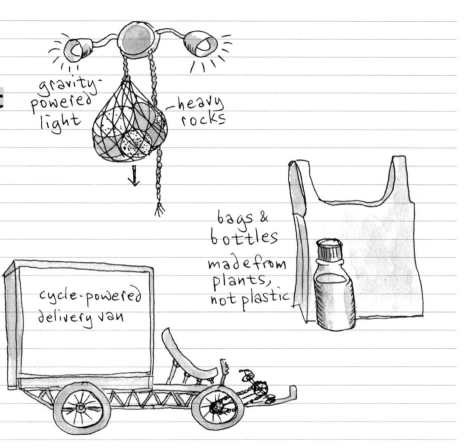

gravity-powered light

—heavy rocks

bags & bottles made from plants, not plastic

cycle-powered delivery van

And of course, talking about climate change helps a lot.

Time to train!

Think of this like a special training session to help you on your mission.

Like the scene in "Raya and the Last Dragon" where Raya's dad teaches her to protect the gem.

Or better yet, the scenes where Moana practices what she'll say to introduce herself to Maui.

Ready? Let's go!

How to teach this stuff:

Use words everyone will understand, even if they don't know a lot about this stuff.

Explain how climate change is causing weird weather.

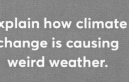

Take your turn listening, too.

After you listen, repeat what you heard. (This will show you care about what the other person thinks.)

Agree on a positive goal, like how you each want a better future.

How does it feel?

A simple experiment kids can do with adults.

People don't always agree or think about things the same way.

So know that this is normal — expecting it can help.

Take deep breaths if you start to feel nervous or frustrated as you listen.

It might help to talk about wacky weather. Weather is something on which most people agree.

These talks don't have to be perfect to make a difference. You just need to begin.

Be ready for different opinions.

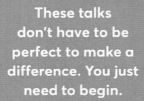

Your mission: **Teach 5 adults**

Alright, it's time to start.

You now have a ton of climate knowledge. You know your stuff. And your voice? It's powerful. *Always has been.*

Time to use both your knowledge and voice to teach five adults about climate change. Let's come up with a game plan, so you can help save our planet!

What is the most useful thing you've learned?

"That I should never give up."

Lucija, age 11, Zurich Switzerland

GAME PLAN
Talk tracker

FOR YOUR MISSION TO TEACH 5 ADULTS.

Start by filling in who you could teach and when. Then track your progress in the last column.

Download this from **thecarbonalmanac. org/genc.**

Completed all of your stars?

YOU DID IT! Here's what to do next:

- Take time to celebrate. You are amazing!

- Visit carbonalmanac.org/genc to get your Changemaker Certificate.

- Let this be the beginning. Let's keep working together to save our planet!

Who you could teach:

Need ideas? Principal, Teacher, Aunt, Uncle, Grandparent, Neighbor, Cousin, Family Friend.

When you could teach them:

Is there a day you'll see them soon? If not, guess when you could teach them!

Did you teach them?

Circle *yes* or *no*. Each time you circle *yes*, color in or check off a star below!

1 _____   _____   **Yes / No**

2 _____   _____   **Yes / No**

3 _____   _____   **Yes / No**

4 _____   _____   **Yes / No**

5 _____   _____   **Yes / No**

Invite others to join this mission!

Pass these cards out at school, stick them on a birthday gift, or hide them somewhere fun for a friend to find.

Download these from **thecarbonalmanac. org/genc**.

SPECIAL INVITATION

Join my planet-saving team!

Get your free copy of *Generation Carbon: It's Time to Start* at **carbonalmanac.org/kids**

 The Carbon Almanac

 Generation Carbon

Ready to learn how you can help save our planet?

Get your free copy of *Generation Carbon: It's Time to Start* at **carbonalmanac.org/kids**

 The Carbon Almanac

 Generation Carbon

The **biggest** difference comes from **acting together with others.**

And remember, the planet doesn't need you to be perfect, → *it just needs you to start.* ←

Carry these lessons with you, and go make a RESPECTFUL ruckus for our planet!

Training session complete!
You've got this.

Kid Contributor Page

Matilde Righi
Age 8, Bologna, Italy

Ivan
Age 8, Minneapolis, MN

Edie Chua
Age 7, Toronto, Canada

Aubrielle
Age 8, Grand Rapids, MI

Lucija Biuk
Age 11, Zurich, Switzerland

Matthew NeJame
Age 15, Boston, Massachusetts

Arlo DeCardenas
Age 18, Fort Worth, Texas

Grace
Age 6, Toronto, Canada

Elizabeth Granger
Age 11, San Francisco, CA

Grayson
Age 5, Detroit, MI

Julia Ankenmann
Age 15, Toronto, Canada

Grown-up Contributor Page

People from all over the world wrote this book.

We had one mission: To spread the word about climate change.

Now it's *your* turn.

Gather your friends and do something that spreads the climate change message.

~~It's time to start.~~ed
We

Adam Powers
AJ Reisman
Allan Ling
Amanda Hsiung-Blodgett
Andrea Hunter
Andrei Ungureanu
Aroop Rayu
Avaleen Morris
Azin
Barbara Orsi
Babet
Bruce E Clark
Bruce Glick
Bruce Macaulay
Bulama Yusuf
Calo Amico
Carl Simpson
Carolanne Petrusiak
Corey Girard
Covington Doan
Darin Simmons
David William Fitzgerald
Desislava Dermishkova
Dorothy Coletta
Elena Madalina Florescu
Etrit Shkreli
Eva Forde
Felice Della Gatta
Fernando Laudares Camargos
Friedrich Blase Blase
Gillian McAinsh
Giuseppe Celestino
Inbar Lee Hyams
Jacqui Phillips
James Tunnicliffe
Jennifer Simpson

Jennifer Myers Chua
Jennifer Hole
Jessica P. Schmid
Jessica Zou
Jodi Levine
Kamilla Cospen
Karen Mullins
Karin Schildknecht
Katharina Tolle
Katherine Palmer
Katie Boyer Clark
Kirsten Campbell
Kristy Sharrow
Laura Shimili
Leah Granger
Leah Phinney
Leekei Tang
Leo Heise
Lindsay Hamilton
Lisa Duncan
Louise Carleton-Gertsch
Louise Karch
Maia Richardson
Manon Doran
Marty Martens
Mary Ann Cabaltera
Mary Elizabeth Sheehan
Max Francis
Mayank Trivedi
Melissa
Mona Tellier
Nicté Rivera
Olimpia
Paige NeJame
Peter Stein
Pieter Visser

Robert Gehorsam
Roc Bata
Ronald Zorrilla
Ross Martin
Sally Olarte
Samantha
Sam Schuffenecker
Sebastien Thiroux
Seth Godin
Simon Davie
Sonal Singh
Stephanie Morrison
Steve Wexler
Sunny Logsdon
Susana Juárez
Tania Marien
Tanvi Muppala
Tobias Welz
Tonya Downing
Warrie Warrie
Winny Knust-Graichen
Yan Tougas
Yve Alecia Smith
Zrinka Zvonarević

Illustrator: Michi Mathias
Designer: boon Lim

Typeface credits:
Turnip, David Jonathan Ross
Averta, Kostas Bartsokas
Jeff Script, Gennady Fridman
Minneapolis, FontPanda

The podcast for curious kids!

"Why is there so much plastic in the ocean?"
"What pollutes the air, and how does it get there?"
"Will the polar bears have enough food because of climate change?"

Hey, Gen C Changemakers! **Generation Carbon** is the podcast where kids like you help grown-ups like us save the planet.

Kids have tough questions about climate change, and you deserve the answers. We'll hear from friends, animals, classrooms, scientists, experts, and changemakers like you. And if you're interested in submitting your own scientific findings for an episode, we need Gen C science-minded reporters on the case!

Visit **thecarbonalmanac.org/genc** for more information, and be sure to subscribe on your podcast app. *Let's change the world, Changemakers!*

→ You can find it on **Apple podcasts**, or **Google podcasts**.

Made in United States
North Haven, CT
16 January 2023

31151607R00040